GRIEF SEQUENCE

GRIEF SEQUENCE

PRAGEETA SHARMA

WAVE BOOKS

SEATTLE/NEW YORK

Published by Wave Books

www.wavepoetry.com

Copyright © 2019 by Prageeta Sharma

Wave Books titles are distributed to the trade by

Consortium Book Sales and Distribution

Phone: 800-283-3572 / SAN 631-760X

Library of Congress Cataloging-in-Publication Data

Names: Sharma, Prageeta, author.

Title: Grief sequence / Prageeta Sharma.

Description: First edition. | Seattle : Wave Books, [2019]

Identifiers: LCCN 2019000629

ISBN 9781940696898 (limited edition hardcover)

ISBN 978194069881 (trade paperback)

Classification: LCC PS3619.H35664 A6 2019 | DDC 811/.6—dc23

LC record available at https://lccn.loc.gov/2019000629

Designed by Crisis

Printed in the United States of America

9 8 7 6 5 4 3 2 1

First Edition

Wave Books 080

SEQUENCES

SEQUENCES WITH TITLES

GLACIER NATIONAL PARK

DREAMING WITHOUT KNOWING

POETRY OBITUARY & NOTES

Not to suppress mourning (suffering) (the stupid notion that time will do away with such a thing) but to change it, transform it, to shift it from a static stage (stasis, obstruction, recurrences of the same thing) to a fluid state.

—Roland Barthes, Mourning Diary

GRIEF SEQUENCE

ON SECLUSION AND LOOKING OUT

after Alice Notley

Seclusion may kill your heart in the process of producing the love-stained stench in your poems, the ones containing boundaries of shame with their sober problems—bits describing loss mirroring its inward entanglements, glow-torches you have never seen before. You light them with two selves and don't wait for anything to flicker false. You can discern the lantern of a falling man, who burned down his desire with tiny humiliated gestures. The mountain peak so high, thus you believe it gives you the one majestic evening you earned. Its embrace is a gentle coercion into wide wilderness: an amenable tyranny of its expansion—grief's artillery to fill all of the black clouds that sallow blue sky, painting it with electric photographic sweeps.

You have to find your strength in this.

COMPLICATED SPIRITUAL GRIEF, PART 1

It was violent and it wasn't. It was violent because it was the kind of cancer to which people refer as beastly, as pure evil, and though I do not really believe in a Christian god or devil, I was left facing one. I am a nonbeliever.

When I faced it, all I had was his past before the cancer and what was leading up to it which led me down his rabbit hole, which may have included a brain tumor and many other tumors. All the spindly parts, tumor-shaped, even things painted for me by his admirers, some faulty, some careless. Spindly grievers. I couldn't look at any of them as they kept metastasizing, but that was an action I knew was not mine to claim but through my affections for my beloved. How could I not love some of his friends or students? How is it that I settle on these feelings as he disappears?

COMPLICATED SPIRITUAL GRIEF, PART 2

Because I am the kind of nonbeliever who believes in the culture around me, I was watching for fragments to arise out of our habits, such as watching *Mad Men* or thinking about madmen, as Dale always said, men who are always falling from buildings out of fear, anguish, alcoholism, a particular self-destruction from self-annihilation—pinhole pains.

Like in Cassavetes's *Husbands*, there were these men: I found his notes for teaching that film and at first I thought it was his personal confession, but it wasn't. It was a list of teaching notes: infidelity, vomiting, being a father, being a husband.

I thought about his sonic piece titled "Sorry About the Rage." I was sorry about it, too.

So what now? I grieve. I lust for company that I can't ask for. I turn into my own madman. Can I do this? Did he enter my body? His energy? Can I be him lusting for himself?

A HUMAN WITH FEELINGS

I am having trouble today. How gauche it is to be in this body being unseen by you now. And I am wearing to bed the floral shirt I bought you, because it's the only thing that keeps me intact. You are not you anymore and I'm trying to understand how a human with feelings disappeared. You were mine. You were floral. You were more than a presence felt. But I fight to find you among the loudest, drunkest voices laughing at me when I go to their bars. Where are you? You held me in so many of them.

UNDER CLOUDS

The only thing I can find to do is mourn my husband like a teenager, downcast, filled with careless intention, crying along a filament of sound in my Converse high-tops, which I believe he, if he could really see me, would love.

I travel to Seattle, now a string of private tree-lined vistas, and forecasts of intermittent, unexpected outbursts and spatterings of rain streaking windows.

It was so clear when he was alive: we had a jaunted and jumbled happiness. We'd drive away from Missoula with the mountains lost in our rearview mirror. Now I am here by myself. It's daunting and full of the solitude of these smaller windows, an ineffable Puget Sound. I understand how the poem can land on its nothing, so the cloudless is somewhere in a spirit that's vanishing on mute.

SEVENTIES LITE & FOURTEEN JOYS & FOURTEEN FURIES

All my life I waited to sing-holler in the bathtub to my own pure dewdrop fury, but it only came with your death and my aching to live out the adequacy of a seventies narrative all the way to its heart-probe pique and loss. I was a margin-cord rammed with storytelling, and with susceptible palpitation to sentimentality in search of a piston: I was sounding out each coarse tangled lyric, unladylike but finding comfort in its seam.

I have been writing to you for such a long time that I stopped writing and began speaking to you. I was speaking to you before you even started drinking your coffee and you kept pleading with me to wait until you finished. "Could you give me a minute? I am listening to you. I listen to every word." It's true. I didn't write poems to you anymore because I have you in my company, and in my company I have you and I have to understand what it means to have your company. Does it mean I just talk to you until you die? Until you don't know what I'm saying and I can't say it anymore?

Is this why I have to write poems now? If I can't talk to you anymore I won't know what to do with myself.

SEQUENCES

LEARNING WITHOUT KNOWING: IMPLICIT

LOVING: EXPLICIT

DYING: EXPLICIT

ORGANIZING: IMPLICIT

INSTITUTIONAL HATE: IMPLICIT

GRIEVING: EXPLICIT

COMPROMISE: IMPLICIT

DREAMING: ORGANIZATIONAL

STAYING IN HOUSE: IMPLICIT

LEAVING HOUSE: EXPLICIT

SEQUENCE: THEN RECURSION

SEQUENCE 1

What is explicit now is that I had been a defenseless dependent
for those years. I wasn't hedging a bet with a life then. I was
just helping myself to it and to the party of coupledom in its
normality, in its rewording of intimate interferences, and to
this one person I loved. I ground life to a powder underfoot,
with the dominion of freedom in front of me. We both did
carelessly then. We shared a living grief of what disturbed us
about others, but it lived only in a grievance and in the exterior
walls. But then this, and I stopped being in those perceptual
truths, of the mind's eye seeing who was where; this was a kind
of luxury of living in knowingness. I gave that up without un-
derstanding I had to. When it does come back I will know I
am healing. What followed? I was struck back up, bent forward
and sprung from my dry hapless complacency. You see, I was
sitting for too long, but at a certain point—I see—I just buckled
and then he quickly slipped into a part of himself that became
part of the hospital. Memories curved and then sounded: were
sibilant and jest, and from not-his-mouth, and not-his-teeth,
and the breath grew so sharp and he grew so thin and gaunt
that he was buried in a slander his body made of him and I
could only spurn cancer as an enemy; nonetheless, it overtook:

13

was inside his brain, his chest, a tumor catching the lymph nodes. And did he tell the doctor he didn't love me anymore and that's why I wasn't allowed into those conversations? Did he want to end with his end and not share it with me? I was a nobody outside of his illness, as was he, but there was no togetherness in there except for something I craved of him and he of me. Perhaps we couldn't do stouthearted with too much talk or we must have really believed we had time: there was not the send-off of which we held each other in the deepness of ourselves, the kind with dramatic northeasterly consciousness. No. It was a disaster of insufficiency that now I learn is what death does with you, if you watch it take out what it needs. It's the power outage with a powdery starch, granules trailing the floor. One foot in front of the other, I have said now to a nobody with me in the laundry room. I spoke out to a nobody that was once him but I don't believe in the idea that he'd even follow me there.

SEQUENCE 2

1) Explicit or Imminent [DEATH OR DYING]

2) I had no warnings only complications.

3) Due to the low incidence of brain metastasis,

4) [DEATH AND DYING] there is generally no requirement for an MRI examination [DEATH AND DYING] of the brain and cervical spine of patients with esophageal cancer; Japanese studies have even opposed the routine brain CT examination of patients with esophageal cancer.

5) [DEATH AND DYING] suggested that with the rapid development of medical imaging technology, particularly the application of MRI and [DEATH OR DYING] the use of enhanced contrast agents in neuroimaging,

6) faster [DEATH AND DYING] and earlier detection of brain metastasis of esophageal carcinoma

7) [DEATH AND DYING] has become possible. Currently [DEATH AND DYING] for the detection and evaluation of tumor lesions, MRI is superior to CT.

8) Therefore, the prompt use of MRI is necessary for the early detection of brainstem [DEATH AND DYING] and spinal cord metastatic lesions.

9) Certain DEATH studies have considered the use of adjuvant [DEATH AND DYING] chemotherapy following the resection of esophageal carcinoma [DEATH AND DYING] to increase the risk of brain metastasis.

10) Implicit or Imminent [DEATH OR DYING] It has been confirmed that the distant metastasis of esophageal cancer [DEATH AND DYING] depends predominantly on the lymphatic and blood systems.

11) The most common pathway for [DEATH AND DYING] brain metastasis of esophageal cancer is hematogenous dissemination through the arterial circulation.

12) In 1940, the Batson venous plexus was proposed [DEATH AND DYING] as a pathway for the brain metastasis of esophageal carcinoma.

13) However, the role of the vertebral venous system in the brain metastasis of esophageal cancers is supported by a more recent study.

14) The present case [DEATH AND DYING] may be more illustrative of the importance of the vertebral vascular system for cerebellar, brainstem, and spinal cord metastases from esophageal cancer, as all three regions are anatomically associated with the same vertebral vascular system,

15) which is distinct from the venous system of the thoracic and lumbar spine and brain.

16) Outcome [DEATH AND DYING] Brain metastases are often treated with multiple therapies, including

17) [DEATH AND DYING] surgery, radiation and chemotherapy. Complete removal of the lesions is the goal of surgical treatment and may improve survival rates. However, this generally only applies to patients with a high KPS score or to those with single, solitary tumors.

18) Academic journal findings do not have a habit of crying out [DEATH AND DYING] among their characterizations of what lies between each hospital visit.

19) I had no warnings only complications.

I know shock takes on many forms and we all become impaired by it. The day we decided on hospice your New York friends arrived. We thought it would be exactly what you needed in saying goodbye, some flicker of recognition from your bed, beyond your restless agitation and the organizational movement of your knees to ankles as you moved side to side. Albeit their flight was delayed and all they could do was complain about the weather and how far away they were from New York City; meanwhile, you were dying right in front of them. We were figuring out whether we'd have hospice in the hospital or at home, but you were convulsing from the steroids that were keeping you quasi-cognizant in your muteness—pupils building into circuits, animated, and we realized we'd need twenty-four-hour care. I was angry with the hospice chaplains coming through, first a Christian then a Buddhist, as if they were looking for the right match for me. I couldn't find comfort in the words of loss. I had no faith to speak of. Your friends in their gaggle: grasped the wrong part of my hostility: they judged: and they decided it was okay to be misogynists to the wife, she deserved it; she hadn't kept up with her looks. One looked for women in the waiting room, eyeing my attractive friend as she served him a sandwich, a salacious up-and-down once-over, and the other went for coffee with your student. He had told you he kissed her on the lips in New York. But what I want to say is that when you were unconscious and dying they told your daughter that there was a reason they didn't attend our wedding back when. After gaining composure and telling me what they said, what they did, how they judged, she declared them gross. She said they only knew you when you were struggling, when you were destitute, when you were beneath them in stature and not being loved wholly by the world you craved. One of them said he knew there was tension in your room when you looked at him with your frown, while dying, and the other believed his voice was soothing, so soothing, like he was a saint, or something. Who is a saint in hospice and who believes in one's own sainthood during this time? When I call this saint for consolation a week later he tells me the worst part of the whole trip was the bronchitis he got: Didn't I realize what he was going through? They were not your friends, I say on this side of the reflection; they ushered in a kind of fallacy of such. They pitied my hostility, girth, and sadness, and thus I pity them who could not see such a light of our family, as we would all say that this is us trying so hard. These are our after-dreams in a hospital having to obliterate our present impaction.

Later, your daughter and I sat at the table; she assessed it from her side and mine, while we had different needs from them; they tried to split what we had to lose into a value that severs all of our grieving into bits, into lost and disloyal friendships, unreasonable strings of what's impassible and petty. We thought about our immediate community, its openhanded emergentness, and how after they left, Ken, our block and tackle, arrived from San Diego, and Dale, closer to the end and slow-quaking, sweetly mute, but offish, lifted his crane arms so slightly and sideways to hug-deep his friend.

SEQUENCE 6

—[In this one] As a kind of lecherous husband who is too affectionate to me, parsing my sleeves, and random people at a restaurant inching toward, and then as we plod through a train station. And yet, he is alive and healthy. It relieves me, but he is always a bit turned-in and drunk, which puts me on edge. We are driving and seeing people come forward into view—with serenity—to greet us. They remain blank and unclear. He exudes a jolly sense of humanness, not bothered by any lack of anonymity.

—[In this one] He and I lived in a kind of Missoula-Brooklyn and we were going to clean the house, but I went to get a pinot noir instead. He started to clean the bookshelves and our entertainment system, full of pollen and dust. This was a light one where Dale and I had some beginnings again, the grain of spots on a photograph. He looked late 40s; he was cheerfully cleaning like a bartender; and then he joined me and picked out a wine from our shop. He wore his gray vest and a pale-color overcoat. It was like we were in a Nan Goldin Dickens novel, he said, but there was happiness above our heads.

—[In this one] We were in a kitchen that didn't look like the one we had. Dale asked me for hot washcloths for him to spit in and I warmed them: different ratty colors. He was sitting by me smoking and for a moment it wasn't him smoking, and I said, "Dale got sick because he was smoking," but then it was him again and I was giving him washcloths. He was shaking his head No.

—[In this one] I read the word *retch*, magnified, and remembered that he started to scare me first with manic drunk hiccups (ten full minutes) that turned to retching, recurring. Till it was a choke, then blood, then he grew into a harmonic shadow-horizontal and also -vertical, and when he tried to say he loved me he told somebody else.

—[In this one] Dale was back. It was because somehow he could live a little longer. There is a hallway light. It is a passageway. We lie together in bed to do this. First, we were in a mountain hospital, Dale asking to look at our vows, which I told him were still in my closet somewhere. We came back to the house that wasn't ours but had all these large jagged books that were three feet tall and upright, and Dale said, "Are you really getting rid of our things?" I said, "I'm just sorting through them." Dale holding tighter than he has strength for, and I said, "I have to be stronger this next year before you go again."

—[In this one] Sick, Alive, Dead, Gasping. Task analysis. Hiding sickness. Hiding emotional affair. Cutting emotional affair off. Diagnosis. Hiding diagnosis. Hiding prognosis. Hiding mortality estimate. Hiding addiction. Hiding cause of death. Multilateral vs. sequencing. Hiding emotional affair till I read an un-erased text after death. Text about love and cuddling not written to me. Hiding impotence for the last five years. Hiding death from me. Hiding ferment. Hiding unconscious states and leaving me behind. Hiding our loved place. Hiding it from both of us. I will dream it back.

—[In this one] I'm exposed and I knew that was the last thing you would ever have wanted for me. To feel so abandoned like a Victorian book. More than I realize you left me to the wolves, but I—as you would say—turned everything to fairy dust. I had to. I found a surreal sea of ochre. I found a way.

SEQUENCE 7

I thought he was overmedicating himself and planning his sui-
cide. I took the pills away from him. He looked defeated. He
said as much. I felt sorry for both of us. His expressions held
this enormity and a seared exhausted center. Spatial discom-
fort started to affect him but didn't take hold till the next day,
when he started to lose consciousness and rattled the house
yelling about thieves, robbers, drunks, and pill snatchers. We
didn't know what was going on: the tumor was rapidly metas-
tasizing its mass through his cerebellum. His body became har-
der to manage and he sprang fearfully through the house tug-
ging violently at his bile-duct tube. Aja and I camped in the
front rooms.

The last night of intimacy, of lucidity—unbeknownst to me—
we sat together huddled and I caressed him, cradling his arms,
his legs, and his penis. I was sure we had time left for more,
but this was the last time he spoke and searched my face and
looked at me with a recognition I understood.

It's how we moved out of consciousness, and I am haunted by
those last days before we succumbed to hospice. I remember

how stunning he was resting in bed—that week before, in our library with a cornflower blue–sheeted bed prepared lovingly by Ashby and Spider. In that bed, an unofficial hospice, he had a look of wonder when we put movies on—he excited over Wilson, the ball in *Cast Away*, and stared unblinkingly at Tom Hanks. We giggled over this, and appreciated how Andrew put the Eno station on next, and Aja lit and framed this sheeted bed with twinkling lamp, an illuminant: bulbs Dale found soothing. We all watched him compose in the air to Philip Glass. I wished that we could have unleashed him to his afterlife then. That's what he would have wanted: a release to his own universe sonant and material, an ethereal ball. An awkward Tom Hanks, a Wilson, and a castaway in a glittering handprinted sea. This death sequence was the one I wanted for him.

SEQUENCES WITH TITLES

PETTY SEQUENCES

Feud. Power. Baking a cake. Risking speaking. Having a voice in the face of annihilation. Anchoring down to not capitulate. The programs feel like "special factories." The meritorious poet. The non-meritorious poet. The cursed English department. The meritorious prose book. The novel. The dead spouse. Verse with captions. The spouse who is alive though dead. The drunken professors. The slurred speech that collective eschews. Communism should be an option, but you still implore success when it's not applicable. We are a sad place. There are no prayers or painkillers for this disparity. We just make a calculable scene and let the students play it out. There is no diversity in spirit. There is a disaster forming and its cloud reaches up before the scarcity falls down in fractured pairs, thus no solidarity among the wounded. It is blinding eyesight. It is the color magenta. It is the hiding of brownish sensibilities. The academic magic was stolen from its civic heart. How I wish there were single principles that were somehow Vedantic. How I wish to shine above these feuds. I wish I could believe you were looking down to manage the wild upkeep of the present as it treads its continuum. The continuing plunked turn. You must have your sneers and sighs in afterlife. I'm still here on earth. Can you believe I'm still in all of what you thought, year two, I'd leave behind? That I would trounce above it like you are in somewhere you might call Byesville.

BETWEEN SIGHS

I am located further inside of this neural obstacle. It is mentally heavy. I organize the memorial service at which your favorite European meal coats the broad corners of the table with crusts and crumbles and rich spreads, olives and such. There are bounty loaves, beveled cheeses, steak tartare, and a filial atonality in the weeping around me. In the speeches. In the stories. So many of our friends, and our colleagues also attend. Museum room alight. One hundred sighs, over and over again. You love it from afar, I think. All occurring within. Family of yours attended. I think with foggy distance of pain: we are a relation through marriage and yet you are the one person of me. We possessed each other, not churched or blocked or fluffed. We were one and now, not. Today I believe somehow, with you dead and me alive, that we evaded church and still received its blessings. I am forming a mental image of numbers and the formal space of time. Sometimes you come back to me complete. Sometimes I just see a yellowish form.

Do you remember our colleague who wouldn't speak to you before you died, maybe three months before, maybe longer? You didn't know you were sick and neither did she. She wouldn't make eye contact, just gave you sharp stares from her incline. She didn't like us then. She scurried into her universe, which was not ours. I had wished she were an imaginary number. I wish it now, too. I want her to ignore me the way she likes to. I wish she would. I pray she will. You must have seen us from your distance, when she came up to me at your memorial and apologized for treating us both so badly these last six years. I was moved by it, but then I learned, several months later, she disparaged me in the same hour, under what kind of heart, with what sentience? I wish I could draw you the lines of selves as they spread out in front of me in their inlets, in their narrow channels, in their division. So the apology was not genuine. I thought this treatment was over, but it wasn't. I was just spared it for a little while.

That other friend sheared me from ideas of loyalty. I found this out later. You predicted it. You would've felt sad and angry for me but you aren't here. You are where your distance lives. You would remind me not to feel sorry for myself because there really is an abundance of friends encircling me. There's no you, I say to you. There's no intercommunication we dilate that is us inside it. I feel you inside but not in space. This is what's devastating. This has been the injurious landscape from which you fled, skillfully sick, what you left me with. I know it wasn't skillful at all, but I want to goad you. I know you didn't want to flee: life meant much those last months. You and I inside of vital functions, some imaginary, some taken to human forms. Some were the last gasps I heard. There is a neural obstacle of one's mind to consider, and I now take my scarf of fear and center it around the bloat of time, of whatever can bring the sequence to the basic character of itself. You might be sitting by me in your distance. I will try to feel the light or manner of this as though you had given me something to put together, a fastening coverlet before we eat or before we go to bed; or to cover your head to feed you what I bought in excess at the grocery store.

This gesture of the overbalanced, the solitary in which I see things lined differently before me now, because it had been stitched from your mouth and gone, so I trudged to look beneath and found I trudge. It's trudging we all do between sighs, I think.

MY POEM FOR MY STEPDAUGHTER

for Aja Sherrard at 20

The portent may itself be memory
WALLACE STEVENS

How hard to carry scores of adults on your back,
not look at them as carrions of need, the distress
of what loyalty requires. This pain is human,
formed from plunges and positions,
misjudged from various heights.

For your love is of a practicalist tucked
under purple quilts, sad conundrums,
under the dearth of too much identity
mixed with middle-class signifiers.
And then some from all other signifiers
like two magicians in someone else's window.

How ceremony
for you was linked to desire, and not to a lie.

What you had is that writing came
from the same plumed pen as your father's.

And when you were writing we took note.
For so long the diary contained a seal depicting a wayward
    sense, descriptions for the sake of describing:

for what? for whom?
Now you're growing—writing is skyward, a future tense.

There is a mountainous place.
It's where my crusty poetry lives,
and where my impulses reach across
the divide to a charted, snowy place.

There is still bewilderment set between our conversations.
Because we wanted you to mature.
Because you see it as our permanent discontent.

Nonetheless, we are close to the stitches where
perfect boundaries darken us to you.

We hope willfully that we are close to the expiration of
    seemingly endless agitation.

Or we are in for years and years of its
wild growth.

How encumbered-now memories existed
before the truth of a portent, which I have always
taken to mean a warning.

MY POEM ABOUT LAST SOUNDS

The summer deck is filling with riotous rain pouring down
from your hands, I think. I'm terrible at these supernatural im-
ages; you wouldn't like it if I kept it up. I know you are trying
to water the plants, and the seedlings and all of everything I
might have neglected for the last three months while I'm here
fucking it all up. You let me sit in my nightgown all day while
I type on the computer under heaps of shitty books. You want
me to move into something meaningful and I know you are a
function of whatever it is because you gave me all the departing
desires, as a way of teaching me to cope and to stay a poet when
I don't feel like being a poet. Now the challenge is in how I put
all this in me in the way you've always presented me with pos-
sibilities, a kind of irreverence. What to do with the heart in
rage. You tend to those plants now—after I've killed them—
and exactly in rain streaming: a figurative blue that pools and
floods damning everything but me with the uncivil domestic-
ity fighting to sound out all the activity no longer between us,
unanswered in time and space. I would tell you every day if I
could that you are still exuberant; meanwhile, there is still time
in the day, I find that the sounds are louder now. I don't hear
you talking to yourself in the hallways late in the evening as

you used to do. It was a robbed mumbling that echoed. Your drink, your vices, the privacy which you spoke to a mute night. I noticed after you were gone that there was no more aurality that started toward a finishing tension: a drone drowned in hollow floors, in a sunburned house, in one now planted with proprietary neglect.

RETURNING TO OUR CREATION MYTH

We were alive in Vinyl Shiraz. Chocolate linen put us into a desire-haze: a room tone of figure eights and twenty-five-song cycles. I knew that truth and I had a certain guarded fullness avow it and a dead emptiness I sealed in bags.

Your bourbon silhouette is what I now touch the curtains with, a love in that. Few knew what separated us. I had no peace. I will say this with an anxiety adjudicated. Corked in a spill. The wine drunk. A tooth soaring. A back splintered. A pain patch.

Your vices were hidden in a city-mouse, of those white-walled Brooklyn rooms—a serrated-edged life-hole you painted us— from the illustrious youth-fueled glow I pulled from scraps and yards: it was a sonic disappearance. You felt shame, you wrote in 2009. You could see an eye of mine sink into a furrow before a stinging temperament blurred our lines of contentment. I knew it was the stupor of the future as it took its hold in your body. You never let me diagnose you.

You always diagnosed yourself, and your death was as sudden as your rage. It rang its own bell to finish. I didn't even realize what happened. I was trying my best to greet your great stride —in its conceit—and stepped away, just as I wanted you to do in my overreaction to the subway platform's creep, but you never did. You loomed and teetered.

Death stepped too close. You always knew where it was and how its night could be summoned; thus that night I didn't feel your spirit lift. You are still here, in some reduction of a silence, I think, but I do not know. I drink whatever raw stillness is left out of the water and grasp a deep hand heartily.

MY POEM ABOUT FALSE FRIENDS

I remember distinct feelings of being the marginalized spouse with two selves seen from the corner of an eye by the likes of you. I was the one that was seen, and also the one who felt a loose grip with that appearance. Your two bro-friends did see me as much less because I was a misshapen bag of stress and feeling the burden of racialized markings. Because of that sort of seeing or not-seeing, you did your best to protect me but you also had traumatic pain to work through. I didn't like some of your friends; I wasn't sure whether you shared secrets with them or they shared secrets with you. Retrospectively, it was all tied to misogyny. You buried yours in your devotion to me, to the conception of devotion as it plays out in long marriages. And yet I banished those friends of yours soon after your death. It was a cathartic gesture, but it caused me a lot of pain. Through its lens I started to question you. What did they think they knew about us? Like Barthes, as I mourn, I am painfully returning to photographs. What they do is sting the inside with nettles of feeling. I will try to feel my way through them as if they are still unburdening me with stereo drift. How can I paint you as flawed when you are no longer here beside me making your case as to why their flaws and yours are something to forgive, even as I sift through a hardened self trying to give you the dignity you asked me for? I will try in this sun. And yet last night in the deep of sleep you came to me and said that the vigil I hold is enough, that what I do to honor and what I do with struggle are the same and that I need to let the misogyny break in its place. If I let the bro–Christmas lights burn out, it will be totally fine, you said.

I've been sad and can't find a seasonal sequence. I go forward then my order reverses and it's winter again, with that sticky ice that lost your footing as you gripped your container of Greek yogurt brought to the doctor's, even when you couldn't speak; only darted your eyes with a fear that continually registered in your pupil size. You clutched your set of things. I see your pink-stained washcloth out from your wool coat. Your cerebellum tumor is inside with your other tumors but I don't know it's there yet and neither do you. It appeared and controlled your brain and the things you couldn't hold. I wonder what things really are, if they are just a set of symbols we sequence and then find purposeful. I wonder whether they are like rituals that we learn for our brain. We have those for our body and those for our brain. I look at you—you are alive— and you breathe labored breaths, and then you died. There, in the hospital bed, when I let time lapse not knowing how to hold you. I let you die for seven days. Your daughter, bigger than I am, could hold you. She could use her muscles to grip you, but I couldn't hold you, even though you lost forty pounds your last month. I couldn't find the sequence because I reversed everything into its pain cycle and you didn't want me to watch you die but I couldn't understand how everyone could let it happen and I could, too, but only if I let it fall into its hole, its awkward sequence, around death. It's not awkward, it's just not right.

I could make many intuitive decisions and as many logical decisions occurred around your treatments, but I didn't know you were stepping out of sequence, and treatments did not produce remedies, and I left myself at the side of the hospital bed. You were in another light, exiting slowly. I thought that accounted grieving would banish all the anxiety, but it came back this year. I became debilitated. I have a debilitating anxiety that I thought was gone. I have too many anxious sequences now and they are blurring meaning. They are blurring my truths like time-lapses and I don't rush to find the joy of the occurrence without looking for the traps, and my logic, and my stumbling out into another bed that places me in this now-future and you don't see me because you are no longer alive with me and I can't rectify this sequence. And I worry that when I love him he will die, too. I can't happen into its learning like it's wisdom. It's still deeply unconscious to hold this fear after I banished worry because I looked it in the eyes and it was real and I felt I knew what it looked like. It's the unknowing learning that I was deeply afraid to imagine, and yet it's your empty bed, your empty closet, you're empty of the spirited you that gave you to me, in that human way we come to rely upon and that shames us so. And every night of this thinking is a long night of this thinking.

Do you fall into bed with us, and I have no idea of this? I'd love to think it's so, and we have room for your sets of things.

I LOOK AT YOUR HANDWRITING

I look at your handwriting, and it pushes space into its narrow field. His were big atmospheric box crosses with architecture. Your speech and talk are the opposite, you have soft, catalectic vowels; his were hard chains of dream-speak. How is this possible? What is richly characterized by handwriting? What is its dictionary of attributes? Where is there an airy space between the way he and I loved? Because then, and suddenly, I loved again. And it arose against sequential time. This makes loving two persons its own council. One followed the other but there is still yet simultaneity; the other loved me but had trouble loving, and I had to absorb this after death. There is loving without knowing and loving with so much knowing: two bodies separate in the night after the coupling of evening-time. One goes up to his room and slowly dies, cigarette after cigarette. After his feeding tube and bile duct were inserted he wouldn't sleep in our bed.

The two broad categories of sequence learning exist—explicit and implicit—with subcategories, which also become dreaming, and reading the handwriting. You were the first person and now you are one person and there is a second person.

Explicit sequence learning has been known and studied since the discovery of sequence learning. However, recently, implicit sequence learning has gained more attention and research. A form of implicit learning, maybe implicit dreaming, maybe a contrary dreaming occurs, maybe dying is more implicit in its sequence; maybe learning refers to the underlying methods of dreaming, or airy spaces or writing words to both beloveds—that contrary people are unaware of what's explicit and what's implicit—in other words, learning without knowing is dreaming.

MY SENSORIAL PROSE POEM

I had these angry flare-ups. I spit out some of them at you as if they were valuable: luminous fireballs running the mile-graves in my mind. Were they winning solvent prizes? No. Not the case. I had to take them out, their markers, their advantageous seats that flicker pain and treachery, bad and cheerless. Because I had to figure out what love was doing in the mix with its gleam of purpose. It was trying to reflect a ray back. It bore a fine, bright will to make more room in my wits. To pull my sensory impulses into reason I need to imagine more affection, which gives me more of you when I carry fondness through all the pallid parts of the mystic brain. Of this mystic year. It won't be colorless. It's too beautiful, and after I sputter its meaning to the purloined, finding the fiery from its heavy furied self I am myself my brain, and it's all of you and him. You both teach me that there is nothing obscure about love that can't be embraced; a sweet-hold, without apprehension, is really what the mystical experience is about. This is what causes the most intoxicating and surfeit mood to settle from cold graphite into a more livable act of survival. It's when the sensory does house memories for the living.

MOURNING

The condo is a dusty library of all the records he left behind that decorated a previous life I had. This morning in bed. "These are amazing," revives me with the recognition that after mourning, there are many mornings that can be amazing: looking out on Seattle and its trees. How they define us and signify our determination. How Seattle, because of its vagueness, provokes us to redefine a squalor. How to read "Some Trees" and see it in the windows acting as trees.

MY NATURE POEM

Started with grass-shaped sickles that stuck out of planks
growing under the blood-rust deck, next to the house.

The air is still blue and its mystery can fill my poem with the
sure density of balsa, its pollen film looming above my head.

I love my natural world even

when I don't travel far into the thick earth of it. It has
its own paper clips that grab me and stick me to its fabric.

Its self-containment suggests that it still can be everywhere.

MY POEM ABOUT NEW FRIENDSHIP

for Sarmeesha

I met you on a party bench at Gita's during that heated lived-out, musty July when I believed only momentarily in both prophecy and its antithesis. You had never met Dale, never knew Dale. You were my friend he would never meet. Alas, I say to quiet us. This is sad but it taught me how real it was to move forward, even in making friends. You were a forehead of zeal and impetuousness—with an inspirited laugh to behold, a danger to my edge—and transatlantic like myself. Just then, you made a cashew hug gesture (signaling how one can give a distant "cashew-shaped" hug); needless to say, we nixed that hug for a long road of intimacy, the abridged version, which was required. We discussed this in clipped sighs accented by beer bottles. Let's not refrain from feeling feelings hosted in newness. Let's celebrate the inanity of being abandoned with vigilance—do the unappeasable by leaving a world of agents and factors who fall down on their faces. I loved your southern chicken curry and I loved that in this loss I have found a deep girlfriend armor. Do not ever lighten my load. You let me be cross. I let you be cross. We give cashew hugs to Missoula, Montana, sometimes: the kind we Indians know how to let loose in tight situations, let this hug modify so much of our shanty-hutch deliberations, and let's make sure everyone knows we're pushy because it's our culture to be such, and when we recoil it's cashew shaped.

GLACIER NATIONAL PARK

GLACIER NATIONAL PARK & THE ELEGY

for Mike, July 2016

After Dale's sudden cancer,

his body wasting swiftly
to death,

I didn't believe in love or beauty, or my
ability to write poems.

And my grieving turned into a sequence of
writing

hostile little elegies
in solitary sittings. Elegies ceased being
elegant.

I guess I was trying to understand

the shape of a new sorrow in its
deep recognition;

how easily it has foraged for my marginalized hungers
that felt

legitimately nullified.

With it, figurative language estranged itself

from crafting mutable metaphors

of the natural world, standing

in its place within adjectival
phrases.

Landscape, though permissible, seemed to only swell around
retaining rivers beneath me with a grave distance
as bodies ensued to ashes,
and I didn't utter *dust to dust*,
and yet only after losing many
months and time
I did (slowly) begin to notice a greener (faint) tint
to the sunlight.
This felt like a
small divinity.

Finding you was this too,
after such importunate abandonment.

I said this is a remarkable lightness I feel. I couldn't imagine
it before I felt it.

You told me to look at the moon.   I did.
That's what you did after Marie died.
And you believed all moons in the sky to be elegiac
or real.
You represented a steadfast truth.

I proposed then a drive to Glacier,
a fine faultless finery—the firs, pines, and stillness.

We drove up—higher than I expected—
up the steepest corners and edges,
and I looked out at spring's sustenance,
an earthwork
of forest trees scored in majestic columns,
bedded and wooded,
coated with needles, fully medicinal,   a simile
of shedding,
of giving over the live forested body
to its eminence.   Of the mountain's height,
its splendor-drop   because of
its scare quality.
I feel hesitant to look out.
But for descriptors: the rounded grass tufts
near the car grates   then a hell-drop,
a belt of green.
Stones and gravel and gray
peeking through.

This driving with you is a climb
of faith, I think,
and I feel it along with

                              a helpless irritation of lust in my
throat and gut,

                              and a pair of calloused and ashen
calves and feet I seem

                              to have earned.
                    You helped me through a dry summer, fall,
winter

          and now   summer.
          Ten months after he died.   He and I, all these years,
          had never gone,
               only near it to Flathead or Whitefish, to fireplace
lodges tucked away.

                                             I brought you to
the Weeping Walls,
               after you drove still farther
               we turned around,
               when I threatened fear of heights.
                         I don't know how to celebrate 100 years
                              this high up but you do,
and you visit
               a winding high-up with me—
                         your glasses cocked on your head,
               a strange visor of blackish hair,
                              camera chest-centered,

erect lens outward but modest,

        two circles looking above my direction

     at the field of bear grass, with its white stalks

and awkward loomed light.

    I was unable to get out of the car at Heavens Peak

because the sublime was frightening,

    but I crawled around the side and peered over, and

I knew

    I would never use the word   *Heaven*

   to describe anything I saw of death, but I needed

       to see beauty understood in a scrap of its

light

         and not be afraid

  of it taking me with it, along the way I had seen him

disappear into illness.

  I must hold you

       where I can see you clearly   and

never plow the hard-won

              truth of pitching

death

    and flinging its burden into spaces.

    No treason I feel,   now (because)

   the eros of the natural world lingers in sentience,

flooding with its central question of what collectively
crushes.

I held on to the silver bumper of your car and clutched
your hand
                because it was   your hand and you, too, were
silvery
                        behind frank light and squinting
                                to see into a camera's moon,
                                        a lingering present
tense
                                we just gave ourselves over to, lifted
to frame
                        its blue course: a formal sky of imperturbable
clouds,
                                of unambiguous secularity.
                                        We take a simple walk by
the car now.

DREAMING WITHOUT KNOWING

MY POEM IN A POETRY HOLE WITH YOU

I've lost good, genuine people for a temporary time when I thought I had to have allegiances that were just false ambitious tantrums. I don't want to do any of it anymore because I really lost too much. More than some of you, casual acquaintances. Poetry can be long and ripe, but it can be puny, too. If it's next to the hole. If it's too close to the gaping hole. This is now where I live, to have some strength in stronger senses of solidarity. To live away from ungenerous arms that grab for power or believe in power. Even writing to a you is too inadequate for me. We must have a large sack of reciprocity. Call it something where you can take it away, and you want me to grovel in its undersized mouth.

I needed so much before I moved to the West. I needed so much after I moved. I don't need the same things after his death.

I write to a larger New York City that I see from a distance. I want to write to a larger good in you, the hole inside of a "gratuitous bag."

I COME SO TOGETHER WHERE YOU ARE

I had a gently gentle touch to give you, and it took me many months to recover it.

It's because death mediated, not just my beloved's, but what made you also widowed and deeply solitary,

keeping you out of yourself in some way I felt, beloved by otherworldliness. You had been loved deeply by another who left you permanently.

I felt this upon our first meeting when my love was alive and yours wasn't. And you had a darkness of such.

*

After his death, I had to travel by Boeing from Missoula to Seattle. You picked me up from the airport when I had ashes in hand. And you let me write to you

when I was in India putting his ashes in the Ganges, and you let me tell you about my cousin's death a month later, who was with me at the Ganges, and he, too, had darkness. But you let me imagine my late husband was in on everything including ushering my cousin to rest, even though you are an atheist, and so am I in many ways, even though I do come so together where you are, and will do this every day, if you'll let me—I come gently with all my unconscious troubles packed.

And I listen to every seventies-lite song for the messages of discovery that draw us away from the unconscious guilted grip and faulty trap

and make me serenade into and out of the halts of beholding you for you to recognize the sound and reasonable influence of the widower-hero you are.

ABIDE

You have gone to get a haircut in Kirkland. But, before you left, you rubbed my arms to warm them, out of the blankets, with a dearness that I thought I would never find. When you grow older and I fret that you, too, will die, you will tell me that I conflate the stars with tombs. I sang you Earth, Wind & Fire's "Reasons" and we folded into the Delfonics' "Didn't I (Blow Your Mind This Time)," and I said you don't even know you did. You are too modest to even think you could and you know somewhere hidden we live now to solve our soft hearts' problems, which come from the fallen places where they are the raconteurs who died on us. They took up the largesse of the art of death, but we don't care who had the better lover, the better spouse, the kinder or more considerate one. Now, we can just take this morning and stretch out a line of aporia, an aphoristic single-sided horizon of trees, buildings, and sky.

YOU LACK FALSEHOOD

What it's like to love again—without apprehension, which I learned to lose because I had to. You with a face of bravery: two softened eyes that suffered city walls and an empty house. You busted bamboo throughout long days of your own wherewithal.

I don't think you understand what I do with you in my head.

I speak to your genuine sense, and my awkward daydream highlights our sunsets to a firefly orange, a dayglow that matches warmth and intensity. This is the enchanting island of your truth upon metaphor: striped shirt, kind single-minded glances, your beauty.

And you, like stars, layer a literality to generate mutual sense, but then your darling torso eggs me on with its charge of heroic build. You lack falsehood, in the way a steeple lacks the largesse of what it represents, the white stature of painted strength, foreign to me, however. But we see it static amid the greenery— trees and brush that cradle your svelte muscle-sense, a former dancer-body to find only grace and health, of which you claim a kind of modesty. But you don't see how you instruct me with the Greek cautionary—pulling the ethics into our silence, and I see this as a kind of interlude between our bodies and our minds and I want to say more to you about the sun's fortitude and yours, but you won't let me do any wayward effusive gestures that describe how you are mythic.

MARCH WIND

I think it's a secret sequence blistering in early spring, found by the patch of snow melting.

We walk by its shine because it's a moon of sorts and we hold our smiles large together. At that moment, I have an insatiable cheer but within an hour it falls into itself like a blanket. It's because if I feel a small change in character, a betrayal by you, even in teasing, I will summon him in to help me out of the present. I become morbid with this because I sense him entering the room—and I can't have you both here—and then I anger at you, because I am ushering him in now, and it feels like a secret I can't share with you; and yet he's so far from me. I am now with you in a little, tiny house. I have a much smaller life in some ways and with less shame than previously. Then I sit with this force of thinking and it turns into an intimacy I can fabricate into significant claims, full of kindness for you, which I have found because if I learn to see it only as hidden from view I manage to get there eventually.

I learn that there are two winters and two early springs happening at the same time and I have to turn one season to the other to get past their painful awakenings. It's just a snow patch. It's still melting.

has removed its glow of intimacy to indecision. Of a hesitance, palpable. Your quiet is pure mood with phantom feelings. Prior to this, we moved rapidly around and around and the whirl stopped you in a cylindrical. Where was the center of this? The *factoria* of touching skin: your beauty of long strength and able warmth. Did you turn it into an indistinguishable prospectus? If we talk about suburban detritus, the debris, the waste—I don't want the detachment signaled in comfortable desultory stares. We had a pulley of love, I thought, and maybe my melodrama haunts all corners of another wasteland, of the dead, out of hearts, you might say, but don't turn us into those long days where I couldn't hold a spot on the wall. I couldn't hold that tall glass of light until I had your body, its invisible traumas and wounds that won't erupt into the voices we muted from speaking their turn, their dead diaries and our live, halting ones full of predisposed descriptions we keep discovering as singular, emerging cautions.

HERMETIC

You said both *hermit* and *hermetic* in the same sentence and I said that if you are receptive then you don't need to be an artist. I have had a hermetic life in poetry and in the sanctity of a sacred love, in one sense but not in another. You said the word *demarcation* and I was reassured by this; how could you understand? I don't think you can.

I don't think you could know what it means to talk your life into its next iteration. This is what I tell my students: grief, like poetry, can move from an Orphic will to a hermetic opulence without anyone giving a shit about it. Poetry and grief are the same: you are taught to care about it when it happens to you. Poetry can happen and so can grief, and particularly the failure of life to death. And it's only this sort of description because I have to let go of all the literary shapes for truth: what we had of real love with its grip, an ice-hold. In the winter when my beloved lost consciousness: he lost all his sentences and I was left many months later holding on to someone else's words for dear life.

Hermit and hermetic, yes, they become one thing, and one thing becomes another, sometimes very quickly but not abruptly. And all unconscious acts are given to us, as are words, and words are simply the utterance of what half-thoughts can look like when we can't help but speak to ourselves, even when despair dissipates for several sweet and nigh hours.

And now I have opened the blue silk curtains and I have seen those words in their entirety demarcate beginnings and endings for almost but not yet a full year.

SEATTLE SUN

There is a quick sharp pull that one might feel, with it a weighted turn to finding brightness where there is none. I have Seattle to thank for this, but the home of the past must be built anew. And yet I am not in my method and have no sense of worship for the work or of erupting into a broken sense, but I am appreciating the copious sunlight with a startled turf-forming consciousness. I must take the fear of normality and the aerodynamics of emotions that fuel the sense of the present and move them to face this now-earned gluttonous love. The wood pulp, the paper, the feeling of how-to-ache of these conditions, and do not permit the imagination to fold into its chamber. How do I turn this summer around? Is there still an I and no You in this problemed space? Can I sort through these offered new moments without your orange pants, your color-blinded syllogisms, and hull of near-end turbulence? I reckon with this now, and the practice of finding the sun to its glory so that the score I settle with sorrow may and must affect germination and tidings thus far.

THE FUNNY OPPOSITE

Sure, I had summers in suburbs, and winters in wildernesses, and autumn in aural configurations where place didn't enhance anything one bit. With the exception of calcified leaves inching toward desecration underneath forceful-walking feet. Spring did announce William Carlos Williams to me, and the "all" felt both integral and intellectually *more important* than how I describe location. I believe now that I am wholly an approximation of something; never quite it, never the whence—not an answer to defeat's culpable treetop nor its contrary antidote, a mown lawn trying its best to glint a kind of deprivation I grant it in my poem, and only here and in the reader's mind. Maybe it's true that poems exhume the pride in our identities, how the landscape of our minds hold more than just figures and their pastoral circumferences, but dear, they give us their place to make the world stunning, a place to breach the contract we hold too close to meaning and fabrication, and from which we are given some of the most imaginative identities on this earth.

POETRY OBITUARY & NOTES

The moon has left the sky, love,
The stars are hiding now,
And frowning on the world, love

PAUL LAURENCE DUNBAR
"Night of Love"

Known for the first half of his life as Eddie and then as Dale for the last twenty-six years.

So he's both Eddie and Dale.

He used to joke to me that "Dale was trying to kill Eddie." Those were his witty and abstract jokes. He loved joking and he loved psychoanalysis, and introduced me to the work of psychoanalyst and poet Adam Phillips. Particularly to the book *Terror and Experts*, with erudite ideas that now help me: "Mourning is immensely reassuring because it convinces us of something we might otherwise easily doubt: our attachment to others."

I am exploring my attachment during this grieving process.

So I am now out a full year and am still very much in a complicated but life-changing grieving process, exploring the notions of narrative and attachment.

These are the facts: I lost my husband, composer and artist Dale Edwin Sherrard, on January 14, 2015, after his fight with esophageal cancer.

This is the fact and narrative, my obituary of his dying days, his death days.

He was brave and stoic during his short fight (two months from diagnosis to his passing) and lost his battle when a brain tumor was found—on January 8—in his cerebellum.

Everyone said that he started to look younger and younger as he was dying: because his cheekbones, smooth and swarthy, were more pronounced and gave him his wild-eyed youth back.

He was devastatingly beautiful (as he was throughout his life, and particularly in his 20s) in his muteness and in-between conscious state: a starry-world quality his eyes possessed— what they might be seeing inside and their outwardness combined with the restlessness of death impending. His breathing—heavy-wind, gusts of heaving—I couldn't bear.

When the oncologist said we should say goodbye, Dale had, at that moment (while having that tumor lodged and obstructing much of his capacity to speak and to seemingly comprehend what was happening), pulled out his feeding tube, as if to say he knew he had to leave us. I couldn't process this gesture. I didn't know how to ascribe the significance. The oncologist said, here it is, he knows what's happening, and I still wasn't sure whether it was a gesture of discomfort (and a reaction to the steroids keeping him alive while we prepared to say good-bye) or a symbolic gesture of greeting the end and of letting go. I was skeptical both of quick assessments and of narrative truths.

At that moment I wished I weren't a poet, because I felt that I had developed a too-sophisticated sense of what the symbolic could hold. I didn't believe it was represented in these gestures. It felt too literal to be symbolic. I believed the body's discomfort somehow overruled the mind's freedom to find and use symbolism. This is something I want to think more about: death, narrative, symbolism, and the end-of-life work we do.

And so we had to say goodbye—unexpectedly—and it was unbearable to let him go. We were hoping we had six months to a year left. I spent those two months fussing and freaking out over his care and advocating for his life and trying to find the right palliative-care doctor, and so I was not prepared to lose him so quickly and unexpectedly. The palliative-care doctor didn't seem to know what was happening—and so couldn't prepare me for the death that was coming. I remember speaking to his oncologist (who finally returned from a holiday break), who said I was right: either he was overmedicated (by the palliative-care doctor from whose care I consequently removed him) or he had a brain tumor. When the tumor was confirmed I felt so angry at myself for diagnosing the possibilities: Did it matter what I had assessed? I didn't want any of it to be true. Did it matter that I suspected his cancer in October when he started to choke on his food? No. What did it teach me? Nothing about reality. Nothing so far had taught me about death. Not even poetry. That is, until I found it during the grieving process.

As a poet I felt at that time hospice had inadequate narratives for me. It made me feel internally and externally hostile toward particular clergy or the social workers, because they were trying to reach me with aphorisms, accessible poetry, and faulty narratives (to me, they felt this way). These aphorisms and their poems felt watered down and basic, not the ones I knew or leaned on besides the poems I taught or read bedside. But then I didn't want any of the bedside poems I had, because they, too, were inadequate. I think back now: I had probably wanted to figure out, mindfully, what were tools and methods poets and artists had to say goodbye, with the kind of grace and articulation they bring to their work, but I didn't have the wherewithal or the forethought, obviously, because of the shock and gravity of the situation. And it didn't matter, really, because I couldn't come up with anything to really say beyond to hold my anger and grief dear and close to me. I couldn't find anything to hold on to except people's arms, and that wasn't enough. And holding Dale while he was losing consciousness was so hard. His eyes looked at me with a fury and strength that hurt my being because I couldn't imagine what he was experiencing and I had to let him go.

During that last week of hospice, my father read from the Vedic scriptures—the Bhagavad Gita—which felt inadequate even though so beautiful, appropriate to the ritual, and required, too; to listen to my dear father, a Hindu priest, who married us and had to conduct the cremation ceremony, and during the ceremony instructed me to put flowers on parts of the body meant only for the wife—how unbearable and lovely and true. And Dale's dear sister Jody washed his body before the ceremony, and his daughter, Aja, held him day in and day out and nursed him tenderly those last months.

I couldn't bear to hold him, and I felt so helpless. I took in the strength of my family and was grateful for the family Dale "Eddie" had given me. I had the bewilderment of feeling—this is because saying goodbye to loved ones is an impossible task and will never have closure. And as I write, I have no grace of poetry here and I feel inadequate as a poet and writer, too. But as I write this I shrug and tell myself that it cannot be helped.

For me, closure happens through talking. Or rather closure isn't closure but openings. I am learning to let Dale guide me through grieving by opening myself up to everything he liked and integrating the attributes of his life and beliefs that gave him joy. Through the grieving process, I've learned to navigate my self-expression differently, and have learned more about myself and about community than I ever thought possible.

We learn so much about our attachment to love and to people. Poetry, I hope, is a kind of learned articulation and sentient expression of attachment to everything we put into it. I hope. I hope to hold love and art, grieving and mourning. All are happening for me now, and I think back to when I couldn't imagine this to be true, one full year ago.

FEBRUARY 2016

LESS MUSIC: NOTES ON POEMS

Poems have found their sources from the following research and definitions:

Contemporary research has revealed that the death of a loved one can elicit a variety of responses in survivors. Psychologically, many bereaved individuals are able to bounce back relatively quickly after the death. Some grievers experience symptoms of grief-related distress (e.g., anguish, sorrow) for a year or more before they are able to incorporate the loss into their lives. Still other bereaved people struggle tremendously in coming to terms with the death or in making a life for themselves without their treasured loved one. This chronic condition, known as complicated grief (CG), prolonged grief disorder, or persistent complex bereavement disorder, is a protracted, debilitating, sometimes life-threatening grief response. CG is characterized by a state of persistent grieving, wherein the mourner experiences profound separation distress, psychologically disturbing and intrusive thoughts of the deceased, and a sense that life is empty and meaningless.

[Excerpted from: "The Inventory of Complicated Spiritual Grief: Assessing Spiritual Crisis Following Loss," by Laurie A. Burke and Robert A. Neimeyer]

sequence n **1** : a hymn in irregular meter between the gradual and Gospel in masses for special occasions (such as Easter) **2** : a continuous or connected series: such as **a** : an extended series of poems united by a single theme <a sonnet *sequence*> **b** : three or more playing cards usually of the same suit in consecutive order of rank **c** : a succession of repetitions of a melodic phrase or harmonic pattern each in a new position **d** : a set of elements ordered so that they can be labeled with the positive integers **e** : the exact order of bases in a nucleic acid or of amino acids in a protein **f** (1) : a succession of related shots or scenes developing a single subject or phase of a film story (2) : episode **3 a** : order of succession **b** : an arrangement of the tenses of successive verbs in a sentence designed to express a coherent relationship especially between main and subordinate parts **4 a** : consequence, result **b** : a subsequent development **5** : continuity of progression <the narrative *sequence*>

"Sequence 2" includes quoted text from "Cerebellar, brainstem and spinal cord metastases from esophageal cancer following radiotherapy: A case report and literature review," by Peng Zhang, Wei Feng, Xiao Zheng, Yue-zhen Wang, and Guo-ping Shan.

ACKNOWLEDGMENTS

Poems—in earlier versions—have been published in the following journals: The Baffler, Poetry, the Poetry Foundation (online), Green Mountains Review, Clockworks (Goddard College), Ploughshares, and Triple Canopy (online).

Thank you, Joshua Beckman and Heidi Broadhead and the editorial board at Wave Books, for your support and guidance. Deep gratitude to Joshua for believing in this book and helping me to navigate the truth and terms of it.

My appreciation for friends and loved ones is bottomless, apparent, and effusive.

Thank you, friends who helped me through the grieving process and supported these poems: Rae Armantrout and Chuck Korkegian, Vera Brunner-Sung and Sam Meister, Don Mee Choi, Anya Cloud, CAConrad, Caroline Crumpacker, Josh Fomon, Stefania Heim and Peter Pihos, Anita Huslin, Didi and Major Jackson, Lisa Jarrett, Katie Kane, Amy and Ashby Kinch, Gabe Lynn, Madison Lynn and Kaley Shumaker, Spider McKnight, Laura Millin and Craig Menteer, Sarmeesha Reddy, Courtney Saunders and Andrew Smith, Kathryn Shanley and David Moore, Jocelyn Siler and Jerry Fetz, Brooke Swaney, Stacy Szymaszek, Dorothy Wang, David Witzling, and Rebecca Wolff. Thank you, dear hearts: Teresa Carmody, Hedya Klein, Katy Lederer, Heather McGowan, and Magdalena Zurawski.

Thank you, Jena Osman, Jennifer Moxley, Steve Evans, Sarah Vap and Todd Fredson, and Douglas Rothschild, for being poetry communities. For giving me sustenance, feedback on poems, and helping me read my work in public settings. Thank you to Mackenzie Cole, Lara Mimosa Montes, Ragna Bley & Triple Canopy, the Poetry Foundation, and The Creative Independent's Thora Siemsen for a lovely interview on grief and writing.

Thank you, Ken White, for reading through many of these poems, providing edits and your imagination and vision for this manuscript, and for so much more: for loving friendship, particularly the strength you gave Dale and me through his sickness and death.

Thank you, University of Montana, for nurturing my writing and community these many years. I have learned so much. During the hardest period, I am grateful for my Family & Medical Leave, and for my colleagues' support of my writing and teaching upon my return, and to the University of Montana poetry students who helped me through with their spirit, brightness, and poems, particularly Max Kaisler and Jordan Chesnut.

Thank you to the University of Iowa Writers' Workshop community (colleagues Brian Blanchfield and Elizabeth Willis) for your support of these poems and your friendship. My students there were a pleasure to get to know, and I thank you for our talks about grieving and living.

Thank you, Kundiman, the Vermont Studio Center, and Naropa University, for your support of my work. Thank you to Pomona College, and to Aaron Kunin, for supporting this work.

Thank you to the Thinking Its Presence board for solidarity and the sharing of trauma, pain, and suffering and making it powerful and creative, and part of our pedagogy.

Thank you to poet mentors who left this world: Eduardo Chirinos, Michael S. Harper, and C. D. Wright. I miss you, and your poems sit inside my poems with light.

Gratitude to my amazing family: Mom, Dad, Manu, Tracy—giving me everything to explore myself and find the same kind of strength each of you have. To Aja Sherrard and Jo Sherrard for all that we endured: Dale taught us to take care of each other.

Affection and everything to Mike Stussy, a maverick editor with a brilliant and unassuming brain, whom I found, another widower in grief. We are finding life together, and it is a blessing.

And always to Dale, the stoic. You departed this world so suddenly and with a swiftness I still can't process.

Tenderness to families who endure the heartbreaking moving forward from cancer, and to the beloved who must face dying alone, amid so much love in the room.